ED SHEERAN

HIS RISE FROM SOFA-SURFER TO MUSIC SUPERSTAR

Written and designed by Gordon Law

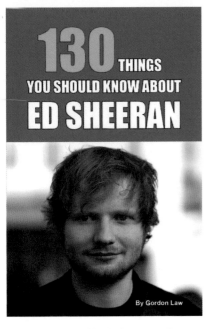

130 THINGS YOU SHOULD KNOW ABOUT ED SHEERAN

By Gordon Law

Also available to buy

ISBN-13: 978-1978120082
ISBN-10: 1978120087

Photos:
Credit for each of the photographs are listed below, with the page on which they appear and location indicator (T-top, B-bottom, L-left, R-right).

Shutterstock: /Christian Bertrand: cover; /Randy Miramontez: back; /Brian Patterson Photos: 1; /Twocoms: 2; /Twocoms: 4; /Featureflash Photo Agency: 5; / brandonht: 6L; /catwalker: 6R; /Peter Jeffreys: 7T; /Martin Charles Hatch: 7B; /360b: 8; /Andrea Raffin: 9; /JStone: 10; /Featureflash Photo Agency: 11; /Paul J Martin: 15B; /Alexander Mazurkevich: 17; /FashionStock.com: 19; /Featureflash Photo Agency: 21; /Kathy Hutchins: 23, 24L; /Mr Pics: 24R; /Featureflash Photo Agency: 25; /Mr Pics: 26; /Featureflash Photo Agency: 30, 31; /JStone: 33; /Christian Bertrand: 34T; /agwilson: 34B; /Featureflash Photo Agency: 35; /Mr Pics: 36; /Christian Bertrand: 37; /Randy Miramontez: 39; /Andrea Raffin: 40; /Featureflash Photo Agency: 41; /FashionStock.com: 42; /JStone: 43T; /Featureflash Photo Agency: 43B; /Tinseltown: 44; /Andrea Raffin: 45; /JStone: 46L; /Joe Seer: 46R; /Tinseltown: 47, 50; /Kathy Hutchins: 52; /JStone: 53T; /Featureflash Photo Agency: 53B; /Mr Pics: 54; /yakub88: 55; /Kathy Hutchins: 56; /Jack Fordyce: 57; /Kathy Hutchins: 58L; /Christian Bertrand: 58R; /Featureflash Photo Agency: 59; /JStone: 61; /Featureflash Photo Agency: 62; /Ga Fullner: 63.
Flickr*: /Graham O Siodhachain: 12, 13; /Peter Morgan: 16; /Karen Roe: 18; /U.S. Embassy London: 20; /Phil King: 27; /Mark Kent: 29; /Disney ABC Television Group: 49; /Mark Kent: 51.
*All images published under terms of the Creative Commons licenoo: https://creativecommons.org/licenses/by/2.0
Norwich Evening News: 14.
Gordon Law: 15T; 22.

Every effort has been made to acknowledge correctly and contact the source and/or copyright holder of each picture and the author apologises for any unintentional errors or omissions that will be corrected in the book.

CONTENTS

INTRODUCTION

Ed Sheeran is one of music's biggest success stories. The flame-haired troubadour is a global superstar, having sold millions of records and becoming an international stadium performer.

Whether he's singing ballads with an acoustic guitar or rapping to hip-hop beats with the aid of a loop pedal, Ed's songs span genres and generations.

His third album ÷ was the fastest-selling by a male artist ever in the UK and Ed broke yet another record by having 16 tracks in the UK top 20.

The record also landed at No.1 in the US, and with multiple songs reaching the top 10 of the Billboard 100, he is a Brit who has genuinely cracked America.

Ed can count two Ivor Novello awards, two Grammys and four BRIT Awards among the many he has already won in such a relatively short career.

Selling out Wembley Stadium and Madison Square Garden three times each as just 'a man and his guitar' can be added to his list of achievements. He's also helped create hits for others too, writing tracks for One Direction, Justin Bieber, Usher and The Weeknd.

The singer-songwriter counts Taylor Swift, Sir Elton John, Harry Styles and other celebrity royalty among his friends and collaborators.

He's a ginger kid with scruffy clothes from Suffolk, and in an industry that's obsessed with image, has become the most unlikely of stars.

Dropping out of school at 16, he moved to London where he played hundreds of open-mic gigs for free and lived on friends' sofas – he even slept rough.

Despite umpteen rejections, Ed has used hard graft and determination – as well as some lucky breaks – to fulfil his dream of being a leading musician.

Not only that, but the awards, sales figures and breathtaking live shows make him one of the most popular – and nicest – singers in the world.

Ed Sheeran poses for a selfie while meeting some of his excited fans.

Ed arriving for 2012's *Ill Manors* world premiere, in London.

CHILDHOOD DAYS

Hebden Bridge in West Yorkshire was where Ed Sheeran was born, but he moved to Suffolk at an early age. He became interested in music by listening to artists like Van Morrison and Bob Dylan.

As a child Ed Sheeran would while away long car journeys with his parents by singing in the back seat with his older brother Matthew.

Van Morrison was often blasted out on repeat, and it was during these road trips that Ed got to know his father's music taste that also included The Beatles, Elton John and Bob Dylan.

Born on February 17, 1991, Ed spent his formative years in the West Yorkshire village of Hebden Bridge, which was once crowned the coolest place to live in Britain by The Times newspaper.

It's picturesque and pretty with independent coffee shops, organic eateries, vintage stores and home to hippies since the 70s.

The market town was recognised for being a quirky haven for artists, musicians and creatives, much like Ed's parents.

John Sheeran is an art curator and lecturer, while Imogen Lock has worked for the National Portrait Gallery and Manchester City Galleries, and also creates her own jewellery.

The family spent many hours travelling to London and Manchester and the regular commute gave Ed an education in music.

When John and Imogen wanted to be closer to their arts consultancy business, the family relocated to the small, rural town of Framlingham, in Suffolk, when Ed was four.

Framlingham is famous for its medieval castle and Ed would sing about this many years later in his hit single *Castle on the Hill*.

There was no TV or games console in the creative Sheeran household as John and Imogen encouraged their sons to paint or play instruments like the cello.

Ed's singing voice started to develop while a member of the church choir and he was also a fairly accomplished piano player.

But it was while watching Eric Clapton perform *Layla* at the Queen's Golden Jubilee concert in the summer of 2002 that got Ed totally mesmerised by the guitar.

So much so that the 11-year-old got his hands on a Stratocaster copy and practiced the song's riff continuously every day.

The budding vocalist's first of many live performances came at a concert at Thomas Mills High secondary school where he played *Layla*.

Ed took guitar lessons after his uncle Bill taught him his first chords and he strummed away for hours on end as his friends played computer games and watched cartoons.

He became fascinated with Eminem's lyrical talent after he got his hands on *The Marshall Mathers LP* and it led to him getting into fellow rappers Dr Dre, DMX and Tupac.

But when Ed first heard *Cannonball* by Irish singer-songwriter Damien Rice, it was to have a profound impact on his future.

Bob Dylan (left) and Van Morrison (above) were some of the first artists Ed listened to while he was growing up.

Ed was born in the West Yorkshire market town of Hebden Bridge in February 1991.

Aged four, Ed moved to Suffolk and Framlingham, which is famous for its medieval castle.

MEETING DAMIEN

Ed Sheeran became a fan of the acoustic singer Damien Rice. When he chatted with the Irishman after his gig in Dublin, it turned out to be a life-changing moment for the youngster.

After Ed Sheeran heard *Cannonball* he rushed out to get a copy of Damien Rice's album *O*.

He was captivated by its sheer emotion and intimacy and listened to it on repeat in his bedroom where he learned all the words and chords.

When Ed's Irish cousin Laura informed him that Damien was playing an under-18s gig in her home city of Dublin, he snapped up tickets and headed over to Whelan's bar with his dad.

Watching Damien command a room for two hours, singing emotional love songs, with just an acoustic guitar was a life-changing moment for Ed.

After the show, he popped into the pub next door and had what proved to be an inspirational chat with Ed. It convinced the 13-year-old to follow a career in music.

An enthusiastic Ed wasted no time in writing his first batch of songs with the basic rhyming sequences you could expect from someone so young.

By Ed's own admission, his early writing was not the best but dad John always gave him support and encouragement. Ed penned his first album *Spinning Man* and most of the songs were about his first love Claire.

Some made it onto his first demo, which was an EP called *The Orange Room* as they were written in his orange-painted bedroom. He burned the tracks on a CD and got 1,000 professionally made.

John took him to see Green Day at Wembley Arena for his first live concert and they also watched the likes of Paul McCartney, Bob Dylan and Eric Clapton perform.

However, it was English folk duo Nizlopi that really grabbed Ed's attention because they performed a combination of his two favourite genres: acoustic and hip-hop.

Made up of singer and guitarist Luke Concannon and human beatbox John Parker on double bass, they are best known for their No.1 song the *JCB* in 2005.

They shunned major record labels to remain independent and Ed travelled all over the country to watch their shows – even skipping school to see his favourite band on stage.

The teenager greatly admired Luke's stage presence and started to develop a similar, traditional folk-singing style to him.

The rap verses and singing choruses used by Nizlopi inspired Ed to start rapping and he penned another tranche of songs in between his school work.

It was at the Shepherd's Bush Empire near the end of 2005 that Ed noticed something unique about Nizlopi's support act, singer Gary Dunne.

Gary was using a loop station, which is piece of kit that allowed him to record and then play back melodies in real-time.

Using a pedal, it lets solo performers sound like they have a live band on stage with them.

Gary was invited to perform at Ed's 15th birthday party and it was here that the Irishman taught him how to master it.

It would take Ed around two years to perfect but he practised at the gigs he played around his neighbourhood in Suffolk.

Ed continued to write music too, putting together a new self-funded EP titled *Ed Sheeran* and selling copies at his live shows and local shops.

Ed's first-ever live concert was US punk rock band Green Day at Wembley.

8

Irish singer-songwriter Damien Rice inspired Ed to forge a career in music.

EARLY INFLUENCES

Growing up listening to a wide variety of artists shaped Ed into the performer he is today. He reveals the acts that had the biggest effect on both his music and his life...

EMINEM

"My uncle bought me *The Marshall Mathers LP* – Eminem's second album – and said he thought this guy was the next Bob Dylan with his storytelling. My parents didn't know what the content on the album was. I must have been nine when it came out. So when you're nine and someone is saying rude stuff, you want to learn it. So I learnt all the album, back to back, and he raps at such a fast pace that my stammer would go when I rapped. That was the speech therapy that cured me, listening to rap music."

NIZLOPI

"This is a band I was obsessed with. I was always front row at the gigs, and after a while, they started noticing me because I would always turn up at the venue at like 2pm and wait in line so I could be front row. They invited me to be their guitar tech on tour and everything from my live set, from the way I control my voice, the way I control the audience, the way I play the guitar, the way I use beatbox, this comes from this band. I'm really, really heavily influenced. They gave me the opportunity to go on tour for the first time and see what a tour's like. I learnt every aspect of my live set from them."

DAMIEN RICE

"Damien Rice is who made me want to write songs. I remember getting home after seeing him and writing four or five songs in a row. They weren't great but I was so inspired by him as an artist. I'd grown up listening to bands and suddenly here's a guy that stands on stage for two hours and captivates an audience. He holds them in the palms of his hands with just songs that he's written on his own and a guitar. There was something about that that really excited me. I could express myself, on my own. I guess that it's back to the lone thing about playing gigs. There was just something that excited me about that, not sharing it with anyone and having it for me."

VAN MORRISON

"He did this album *Irish Heartbeat* with The Chieftains. I come from an Irish family and spent most of my childhood summers, birthdays and Christmases in Ireland listening to trad music and this was a record that my dad played a lot. *Carrickfergus* is probably one of my favourite songs in general in life, but hearing Van Morrison sing it is pretty wonderful."

Eminem caught Ed's attention at the age of nine and he learnt to rap each of his songs.

Ed at the Capital Radio Summertime Ball, at Wembley, in 2012.

ERIC CLAPTON

"It was the Queen's Golden Jubilee in 2002 and I remember watching it and this guy came on stage with a graffiti-splashed guitar and played this riff. I said, 'Dad, who played that?'. He said it was Eric Clapton and I was, 'Wow!'. The riff just stuck in my mind and that day I said I want to be a musician, I want to play guitar. So I got a guitar for Christmas and it was the first song I learnt and the only song I could play for a long time. I just played that riff over and over again. He's such a fantastic man and I'm learning more and more every time I see him."

GROWING UP FAST

When he wasn't doing school work, Ed would pick up his guitar and perform at local gigs. He was a big fan of English folk duo Nizlopi and they helped with his music education.

School life wasn't always easy for Ed Sheeran as his red hair and big glasses made him a target for bullies while he also had a stammer and hearing problems.

Ed claims he developed the speech impediment as a young kid after he underwent laser surgery to remove a port-wine birthmark on his face.

He managed to overcome the stutter by imitating Eminem's fast-paced rap lyrics.

Like many of his peers, Ed was into rockers Linkin Park, Blink-182, Green Day and The Offspring, but nobody wanted to form a band with "a really geeky ginger kid with spectacles" as Ed later described himself.

Undeterred, Ed continued to perform on his own with just his guitar and loop pedal at family weddings and local venues around Suffolk.

As one of the early pioneers of social media, he started to build up a loyal following of fans through the music networking site MySpace.

Ed then became interested in American guitarist Preston Reed, who could make percussive effects just by tapping and slapping the strings and body of his guitar with his hands.

The teenager headed to Scotland for a five-day summer workshop and was taught some of these techniques.

He would even hone his singing voice by busking in Galway while on a family holiday in Ireland.

Homework was put aside in favour of performing at local gigs but his parents John and Imogen were always there to support him wherever he went.

Ed loved singing and playing music but he enjoyed treading the boards too.

He showed off his acting prowess in school productions of *West Side Story*, *Grease* and *The Sound of Music* and joined the London-based National Youth Theatre at 15.

There was a two-week audition for a new ITV musical drama series called *Britannia High* which required youngsters to be able to sing, dance and act.

Though Ed reached the final four, he failed to impress the judges and missed out on appearing in the show, which was similar to *High School Musical* and *Fame*.

At this point Ed decided to give up on the idea of becoming an actor and focus on a career in music instead.

Ed emailed Nizlopi a song he wrote in tribute to them titled *Two Blokes and a Double Bass* and was overjoyed when his hero Luke Concannon replied back.

He kept in touch with Nizlopi and was offered a job as their guitar technician for their upcoming summer tour. From the end of 2006 and early 2007, he set up their equipment and changed their strings.

Here he experienced first-hand how a professional band wrote songs, performed live and interacted with the fans.

His next decision was working out whether to stay at school and take his A-levels or aim to become a music star.

When the 16-year-old opened for Nizlopi at his home-town venue of the Norwich Arts Centre, Ed's mind was made up.

Ed enjoyed watching Nizlopi's John Parker play the double bass.

Nizlopi's lead vocalist Luke Concannon was another singer Ed looked up to.

LONDON CALLING

At the age of 16, Ed left the Suffolk countryside and moved to the capital to get songwriting experience. Here he performed at many venues across the city, but it wasn't always easy.

Ed Sheeran logged in to his MySpace page and noticed a private message that caught his eye. A music manager had got in touch after he liked one of the songs on the website from Ed's latest EP *Want Some?*. He followed that up by arranging some songwriting sessions for Ed in London.

That opportunity was all Ed needed for him to quit education, and with the support of his parents, head to the capital at the age of 16.

Ed reckoned that if it didn't work out, he could always go back to school the following year.

With his lightweight Martin Backpacker guitar and loop pedal in his rucksack, Ed ventured south and stayed on the couch of a friend or the music manager.

He then went back to school – the Access To Music college, in east London – to take its Artists Development course for two days a week.

As his parents' salary was below the minimum threshold, Ed was given a government grant of £400 a month which covered his rent for the year.

The college would give Ed an opportunity to learn a set of skills such as audience analysis and marketing to help grow his career.

Ed got to work straight away, emailing more than 300 London promoters that put on acoustic nights and he got around 50 replies back.

Ed performed his first London gig at the upstairs room of the Camden Head (then known as The Liberties) and was so excited that he gave away free copies of his CDs at the end of the night.

He would sometimes play at two or three different shows a day – often filling in for acts who failed to turn up – and didn't get paid. Well, in money at least. Instead, Ed was rewarded in beer or shots of tequila.

Playing at different open-mic venues, from comedy to acoustic nights, Ed exposed himself to a wide range of audiences and it was a steep learning experience.

He lived off the proceeds of the *Want Some?* and *Ed Sheeran* CDs he sold at the back of the gigs which covered his food and travel costs.

On some occasions, Ed would play in front of just a handful of people but he refused to give up and continued to gig almost every day.

When the music course finished in the summer of 2008, so did the grant that had paid for his rent. He had no option but to move out of his flat-share.

He formed a group of friends that played gigs together and they let him crash on their sofas, which was something he did until the end of 2010.

The 17-year-old went back to eastern England to enter the 2008 Next Big Thing talent contest.

Despite breaking four guitar strings and suffering problems with his mic, Ed came out victorious, claiming a cash prize, studio time and music equipment.

With the highs, came the lows, and back in London Ed often wandered through parts of the city late at night after gigs with nowhere to sleep.

There were times Ed had naps on London Underground trains to keep warm and he even spent nights sleeping rough outside Buckingham Palace.

A typical day would be waking up at a random spot, heading off to a session, playing at a gig, have drinks afterwards and then find somewhere to sleep.

Ed was totally skint but he was doing what he loved and was happy.

Ed proves he's the Next Big Thing

A teenage Ed showed his potential as a singer by winning a 2008 talent contest.

The Camden Head pub was where Ed played his first-ever gig in London.

Ed often slept outside Buckingham Palace when he had nowhere to crash for the night.

TAKING SMALL STEPS

Ed sang at various London pubs and clubs almost every day. He met some notable figures in the music industry who helped him edge ever closer to realising his dream.

Despite gigging tirelessly, Ed Sheeran had still not been picked up by a record label – but he had a master plan to change that.

Ed's strategy was to release a series of five self-funded EPs to demonstrate his wide-ranging musical ability.

There would be one showcasing his talent as a singer-songwriter, one covering folk, one indie, a live one and finally one with collaborations.

His management company hooked him up in 2009 with hip-hop producer Jake Gosling who was working on London rapper Wiley's album.

Ed connected with Jake instantly and the pair wrote and recorded together at his studios in Windlesham, Surrey.

They put together the five-track *You Need Me* EP and Gosling let Ed crash at his house. A re-worked version of the title track would go onto become one of Ed's most recognisable songs.

Ed's manager then packed him off to Pontypridd, in South Wales, where he met singer-songwriter Amy Wadge, who was tasked with sharpening his writing skills.

She was blown away by Ed's raw talent as the duo wrote seven songs over two days and some would appear on his *Songs I Wrote With Amy* EP.

Ed entered the 2009 Island Record contest to find the best new artist – and he was triumphant, winning studio time and a deal to release a single *Let it Out*.

However, Ed failed to impress the record company who didn't even bother to watch him play live and they let him go.

Despite minor progress, Ed was frustrated at playing the same old gigs and being told by music execs to change his look, quit rapping and to stop using a loop pedal.

He rejected this advice because he wanted to just be himself and play the music he and the fans enjoyed. So he walked away from his management company.

The singer decided that investing in his education may help his advancement in the industry, so he decided to enrol at university in Guildford to study music.

A promoter friend, who had been doing gigs with Ed for years, offered him a support slot on Just Jack's forthcoming tour. The London pop star, who sang the hit *Starz in Their Eyes* in 2007, was on Elton John's Rocket Music record label.

Opening for Just Jack and playing at the likes of the Shepherd's Bush Empire was a thrilling experience for Ed, especially after seeing his heroes Nizlopi play there when he was 14.

While touring, Ed met Stuart Camp from Rocket Music Management, which was run by Elton John, and he signed with them. In typical Ed fashion, he ended up living on Stuart's sofa.

Despite having a new manager, Ed was still knocked back by the likes of Sony, EMI and Island and he became deeply frustrated by the rejection.

He continued gigging and even resorted to performing at people's houses where food and a bed came as part of the payment.

Around the Christmas period, Ed was asked to play a gig at a warehouse for Crisis Shelter Homeless. He met a girl named Angel and was shocked at how bad life was for her and others who lived on the street.

Later that night at his Guildford flat, Ed wrote his breakthrough song *The A Team*.

Ed had achieved his goal of playing 300 gigs throughout 2009 (reportedly 312 in fact) after he was inspired by James Morrison doing 200 in a single year and got signed. But could Ed?

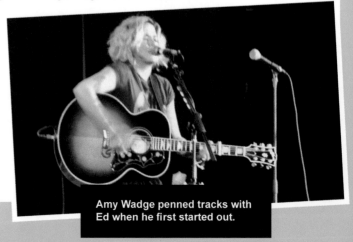

Amy Wadge penned tracks with Ed when he first started out.

Elton John's management company signed Ed after spotting his talent.

DID YOU KNOW...?

**So you think you know everything about Ed Sheeran?
Check out these fun facts on the flame-haired musician.**

1 Along with his cameo in *Game of Thrones*, Ed has also appeared on: New Zealand soap *Shortland Street*; medieval drama *The Bastard Executioner*; US sitcom *Undateable* and Aussie show *Home and Away*, plus the film *Bridget Jones's Baby*.

2 Trevor, Keith, Lloyd, Nigel, Cyril, Felix and James the Second are names given to Ed's guitars.

3 Gordon Burns, presenter of 80s' game show *The Krypton Factor*, is Ed's second cousin.

4 Ed fit 55 Maltesers in his mouth while appearing on James Corden's *Carpool Karaoke*, beating his previous record of 40 set when he was a teenager in a YouTube video.

5 One of Ed's cousins, Jethro Sheeran, is a rapper who goes by the stage name Alonestar and worked with him on some tracks.

6 Granddad Bill used to be an amateur boxer and was involved with the British Boxing Board of Control.

7 He appeared on *The Voice USA* to help Christina Aguilera mentor contestants in 2013.

8 Ed has penned songs for a number of acts which includes: One Direction, Taylor Swift, The Weeknd, Jessie Ware, Rudimental, Usher, Justin Bieber, Major Lazer, Hilary Duff, Robbie Williams and Olly Murs.

9 A pig-shaped statue, named 'Ed Sheer-Ham' was unveiled as part of a Pigs Gone Wild art trail in Ipswich in 2016. Ed bought it for £6,200 at a charity auction with proceeds going to the local hospice.

10 Ed introduced *Friends* star Courteney Cox to future fiance Johnny McDaid of Snow Patrol.

11 GQ magazine honoured Ed with the Worst Dressed Man award in 2012. "Named no.1 worst dressed male in GQ, glad they noticed. I did wear a Burberry suit once," he tweeted at the time.

12 Restaurant chain Nando's created a special 'Ed's Peri-Peri Sauce' with Ed's face on it.

13 After learning his first guitar chords, *A Million Miles Away* by Rory Gallagher was the first song Ed learned to play fully.

14 Ed has been given the title of Baron von Edward Sheeran of Sealand by the independent state of Sealand, which is located in the sea off East Anglia.

15 Older brother Matthew is an award-winning classical music composer who specialises in music for film and TV.

16 Robinsons Fruit & Barley squash is Ed's favourite drink and he requests it for his tour rider.

17 Ed's childhood friend Phillip Butah produced the artwork for his albums and also an illustrated book of his life. Ed's art consultant parents have worked with Phillip since he was 15 years old.

18 As a child, Ed played the cello and also the piano, attaining grade five at the age of eight. However, these days he no longer tickles the ivories.

19 Ed has been immortalised in wax at Madame Tussauds in the USA.

20 Some of his songs have appeared on TV shows, including: *Make It Rain* in *Sons of Anarchy*; *I Will Take You Home* in *Cougar Town*; plus *All of the Stars* for the movie *The Fault in Our Stars*.

Ed performs on the runway at the annual Victoria's Secret fashion show at Earls Court in 2014.

AN URBAN DEVELOPMENT

While Ed continued to play at many gigs, he made efforts to reach a new audience in the UK rap scene. Posting videos online was a plan to give his songs maximum exposure.

Ed Sheeran was an expert at using the power of social media to promote his songs.

He had already built up a growing network of fans on MySpace and that led to a music manager setting up writing sessions for him in London.

The internet-savvy Ed also produced videos for his songs and uploaded them to YouTube to get more people to hear his music.

And in early 2010, an exchange on Twitter led to him being invited to appear on urban music channel SBTV which promoted rising grime stars like Wretch 32, Ghetts and Labrinth.

Jamal Edwards, who founded the YouTube channel, was impressed that Ed could not only sing and play guitar but rap and beatbox too.

Ed was the first non-rapper to appear on SBTV which filmed him performing *The A Team* and *You Need Me, I Don't Need You* along with a Nizlopi song.

This was another big moment for Ed because the videos – and several more he would release over the year – became viral and helped introduce him to a new genre of fans.

Though his gigs were popular, Ed was still struggling to make ends meet and wondered if he'd ever make it as a big-name singer.

Back in the studio, Ed and Jake Gosling produced his next EP titled *Loose Change* which featured standout track *The A Team*.

It sold enough copies for Ed to fund the third of his five-EP collection called *Songs I Wrote With Amy*.

Using tracks he and Amy Wadge had written in Wales two years earlier, Amy also added her vocals to it. Ed's friend, actress Selina MacDonald, knew a photographer who wanted to produce *The A Team* video for him.

Selina offered to play the role of Angel from the song and the entire video cost Ed £20 – the price of some fishnet tights and a crack pipe.

Another mate of his had a contact who ran an open-mic poetry night in Los Angeles and organised for Ed to appear on the evening's line-up.

Ed planned to get a writing session with James Bourne from Busted, who he knew through a mutual friend, while out there at the same time.

So in April 2010, the 19-year-old scraped together all the cash he had earned from CD sales, packed his bags and booked a flight to the USA.

Jamal Edwards, from urban online music channel SBTV, gave Ed a platform to promote himself when he was trying to break through.

London rapper Wretch 32 regularly featured on SBTV and later collaborated with Ed.

COMING TO AMERICA

When Ed flew over to Los Angeles, he ended up hanging out with Jamie Foxx. But would that chance meeting with the Hollywood actor help launch Ed to music stardom?

Standing at the side of the stage before his first-ever gig in the US, you could understand if Ed Sheeran felt a sense of trepidation.

The Flypoet night was held at The Savoy Entertainment Center, based in the Los Angeles suburb of Inglewood, which has a reputation for being a rough part of town.

The room was made up of a largely black audience and a white ginger kid from England was the only acoustic act on a night of comedy and poetry performers.

The crowd didn't know what to make of Ed at first as he entered the stage with his little guitar and started singing *You Need Me, I Don't Need You*.

But when he dropped in lyrics from 50 Cent's *In Da Club* and then invited members of the audience join him on stage to rap with him, the place went wild.

Ed said the reaction he got was his best yet and he earned $700 from selling EPs out of his bag at the back of the venue.

The singer made such an impression, the club's promoter helped secure him a gig at Hollywood actor Jamie Foxx's club, The Foxxhole, based in downtown LA.

It was here that Jamie's manager watched a breathtaking performance by Ed and was waxing lyrical to him afterwards. He invited Ed to Jamie's satellite radio music and comedy show.

Again performing *You Need Me, I don't Need You*, Ed went down a storm, dropping in lines from Jamie's own song *Winner* that had him singing along too.

A few days later, the star emailed Ed inviting him to stay at his mansion in the Hollywood hills where he could use his studio for free and Ed recorded tracks *U.N.I* and *Wake Me Up*.

Ed camped out on the Oscar and Grammy winner's studio couch – and it was probably the most expensive one he had ever slept on.

It was a friendly atmosphere in the Foxx household and Ed spent time hanging out with his family, even jamming on a guitar with his daughter.

Ed continued to play at urban nights around LA and was able to sofa-surf at the various promoters and music managers he met.

The record labels in the UK had rejected Ed but Jamie offered him a deal and even Oprah was interested in signing him up.

Ed found a new sense of confidence and belief and felt that maybe he was about to finally get recognition on his return to England.

Ed travelled to Los Angeles to play at The Savoy Entertainment Center in Inglewood.

Hollywood actor Jamie Foxx was so impressed by Ed's ability that he let him stay at his house to record music.

SETTING AN EXAMPLE

Securing a support slot with a chart-topper like Example was vital in raising Ed's profile. He also returned to the studio to produce EPs that would showcase his varied musical ability.

Ed Sheeran's first gig back in England was at a school fashion show in Suffolk.

It was a big comedown from recording music while living at Jamie Foxx's house.

The experience in LA taught Ed that in order to stand out from the crowd, he needed to stop playing acoustic nights.

Playing love songs at rap, soul and comedy shows in London was Ed's new direction and he enjoyed winning over an audience used to a totally different genre.

This helped Ed get to know rappers involved in the UK grime circuit – and he then spotted an unlikely opportunity on social media.

Pop-rapper Example tweeted that he needed a support act, so Ed thought it would do no harm in tweeting back his interest.

After Ed sent a link to his SBTV video, Example became an instant fan and got Ed to open for him at his first gig in Norwich.

When the band that was due to support Example quit, he chose Ed to take the stage first for the rest of his tour.

Ed and Example ended up becoming good friends and the pair even recorded little ditty *The Nando's Skank* on YouTube, praising the fast-food chain of the same name. The idea was that Ed could claim an elusive 'black card' which enabled holders like Example free food at their restaurants.

The plan worked with the company uploading the video to their Facebook page and Ed got himself a card. Ed now had a regular supply of peri-peri chicken and chips to ensure he never went hungry.

A booking manager was now getting Ed regular gigs around the country and he was at last receiving payment for playing.

Ed continued with the fourth of his five independent EPs: *Live at the Bedford* to flaunt his skills as a live performer in October 2010.

He recorded and filmed his set with a full band The Remedies at one of his favourite venues, The Bedford pub, in south London, where he had been a regular performer.

Ed put the finishing touches to the last of his collection of five EPs, recorded with the aim that it would create enough hype for a recording contract.

No.5 Collaborations Project featured a collection of the leading lights of the UK grime scene such as Wiley, JME, P Money, Ghetts, Devlin and Wretch 32 over eight tracks.

UK grime artists Ghetts (above) and Wiley (right) teamed up with Ed for his *No.5 Collaborations Project* EP.

Rapper Example asked Ed to open for him on his UK tour.

25

THE BIG MOMENT

There were occasions when Ed felt he was never going to be signed by a record label. But he hoped that if he kept playing gigs and releasing good music, eventually his time would come.

When Ed Sheeran went along to watch Bruno Mars in concert he could never have imagined it would lead to his biggest break yet.

After the show in London's Notting Hill, one of Ed's fans spotted him in the crowd, introduced him to her boyfriend, and they went back to their place to listen to music.

During the evening, Ed put on a demo of his *No.5 Collaborations Project* and unbeknown to him, the girl's partner was an A&R for Asylum-Atlantic Records.

The talent scout loved what he heard and started watching Ed's gigs around London, even venturing to Norwich for his sold-out Waterfront show.

But as 2010 closed out, and despite performing at multiple shows, Ed again started to become very frustrated with how everything was going.

Having done hundreds of events and released four EPs, Ed still had little money, no place to live and had made tiny progress over the past three years.

One night, having finished a gig and walked for more than two hours with no money for a taxi and a dead phone battery, it all got too much for Ed.

When he finally got to his friend's place, Ed sat on the sofa and broke down in tears. He felt like jacking it all in there and then.

It didn't help that one particular record label rejected his *No.5 Collaborations Project* EP and even suggested that he give it away for free. However, Ed refused to quit and knew he had to remain patient if he was to get signed.

Ed put all his singles and EPs on iTunes worldwide and they were selling well, with around 10,000 copies downloaded, which had got them into the iTunes chart.

The singer released *No.5 Collaborations Project* on iTunes in January 2011 and was expecting it to get to around number 50.

But over the course of the week, Ed's supporters came out in their thousands to download it and Ed was staggered when it ended up at number two.

Ed wanted to have 'No.5' in the title so people would seek out the previous four EPs and the plan worked as the other records climbed the iTunes chart.

At this point Ed was getting multiple calls from an unknown number before he got a text from manager Stuart Camp telling him to pick up the phone.

It was Elton John – the boss of his management company – who was calling to congratulate him on the EP's success.

All the record labels that had shunned Ed and 'No.5' before were now desperate to sign him, with some offering Ed up to £200,000.

Ed opted for Asylum-Atlantic; not because it was the only company who hadn't rejected him before, but they actually made the effort to watch him live.

The label submitted just £20,000, which was the

Ed rejected many record companies to sign with Asylum-Atlantic.

Ed performs at the Dot to Dot Festival in Manchester, in May 2011, in one of his first gigs since being signed.

lowest out of them all, but Ed was impressed with how they nurtured talent like James Blunt, Plan B and Jess Glynne.

When Ed checked the balance for the songs he sold on iTunes, Napster and Amazon, he was gobsmacked – it was around $500,000.

Ed could earn decent money as an independent artist, but he reckoned the label would give him worldwide TV and radio exposure.

This, in turn, could lead to him selling millions of records, play at big stadium arenas and catapult Ed into a major star. It was a no-brainer.

He removed his songs from iTunes and paid off his parents' mortgage with the proceeds. After four years grafting at gigs all over the UK, releasing songs and sleeping on people's sofas, Ed finally got a recording deal.

With hundreds of thousands of followers built up over years on Twitter, MySpace and Facebook, he had a loyal fan base like no other unsigned act.

Ed's independent EPs proved his talent, and having had companies fight over him, he was in the strong position where he could dictate the music he would produce.

ED'S SUCCESS TIPS

Ed Sheeran achieved his dream of becoming a professional singer. Here's his blueprint to be a winner in music and anything else...

SET GOALS

"I have to have new things to aim for. The last peak on the last album was to play Wembley once and we ended up doing it three times. The peak on the album before was doing Madison Square Garden once and I did it three times. The peak before that was to do Shepherd's Bush [Empire] and sell 100,000 [albums]. I think you need to choose someone that's at the top of their game [as a benchmark]. I probably won't sell 20 million records. And I probably won't ever be as big as Adele. But if you don't aim for the top of the mountain, how are you ever going to get halfway?"

MAKE YOUR OWN LUCK

"Luck is circumstance, how you put yourself in certain positions and how you work yourself in and out of those positions. Luck is a mixture between work ethic, circumstance and people helping you. I've been very lucky to come across some very nice people, but if I hadn't been doing three gigs a night, maybe I wouldn't have bumped into them."

FIND MENTORS

"Luke Concannon [from Nizlopi] is my childhood hero, I grew up listening to him. I went on tour with him, doing guitar tech-ing and learnt everything there is to know about performing, writing, singing, playing guitar, everything. I owe a large amount of my career to him."

DON'T FEAR FAILURE

"I thought I couldn't do an arena and when I did an arena and it was fine, I was like, 'I might as well try Wembley. What's the worst that could happen?' The worst that can happen is you fail. But you still sold Wembley. The worst that can happen is you fail and you move back to the arenas. If you fail, you've not lost anything. But if you achieve, and make it good, the possibilities are endless."

BE A NICE PERSON

"What I've learned about music today is no one has to buy your record any more. Usually they'll buy your record if you're a likeable person. Adele's incredibly likeable, as is Taylor [Swift], Bruno Mars, Sam Smith. I'd like to think that I was likeable. You'll find kids, instead of illegally downloading the album because they want to hear it, they'll be like, 'Oh I think they're a nice person, I'm going to support that' and then they'll go and buy the album. I've never been disproven because anyone that comes across as a dick does not sell that many records. I've found that everyone who is at a certain [high] level, they're all nice."

PRACTICE, PRACTICE, PRACTICE

"I'm proof that people aren't born with talent. If you listen to my early recordings, I can't play guitar and I can't really sing or write music very well either. It's all come through practice. You start off with a little spark and it's whether or not you nurture that spark. You have to expand it and work on it. I sang in the choir at school. At first I couldn't sing at all, but I improved with regular practice... I read [the theory that it takes 10,000 hours of doing anything to master it] when I was 13, John Mayer used to talk about it. I think it's true. I'm coming up to 10,000 hours and I'm now a professional musician. So it definitely does work."

WORK HARD

"I've always had an ethos of just working harder than anyone else I admire and respect and trying to be nice. My dad always told me to choose someone you admire and work harder and be nice to them. So when I signed to Atlantic Records, I saw that James Blunt had sold 10 million records in *Back to Bedlam*. So I said to Atlantic Records, I want his diary of that year and so I took the diary of everything he had done that year and we doubled it. We ended up selling half as much but then on this record now we sold more, so it's working."

Ed sings at one of his record-breaking Wembley Stadium shows.

BE YOURSELF

"There is no one that's going to write songs like you and there's no one who is going to sing like you, as long as you keep it exactly yourself. Imitate people to a point to get your influence and help you write songs, help you learn guitar and help you learn to sing. But once you've found your voice, do that and just stick with it. Even if it sounds odd and people are telling you it won't work, just stick with it and eventually it will. There's seven billion people in the world and there's bound to be one person that likes your music."

LOTS OF PLUS POINTS

With his newly signed record deal, Ed unveiled his debut studio album to the world. Ed knew he could count upon his legion of fans to help drive the record up the charts.

As Ed Sheeran embarked on his debut studio album, he now had a heavyweight record label behind him for the first time.

There was now a team of professionals to do the work that Ed had to do on his own before, like arrange media interviews, upload videos and track sales figures.

The maiden LP was titled with the symbol + (pronounced 'plus') and most of it consisted of love songs about Ed's ex-girlfriend Alice.

They had already been written and recorded over the years and Ed reunited with Jake Gosling, while there was additional production from US hip-hop producer No ID and Charlie Hugall.

Arranged by Asylum-Atlantic, Ed performed *The A Team* on BBC show *Later… With Jools Holland*, and in doing so, achieved one of his life-long ambitions, which marked a significant moment in his career.

The A Team had been a track used on Ed's *Loose Change* EP and it was chosen for his first single in a June 2011 release. The accompanying video was already on YouTube where it had garnered more than one million views.

However, Radio 1 was reluctant to play the song as it felt it was not suitable for its target audience of younger listeners – but Ed had an idea to win them around.

He tweeted that he was playing a free gig at The Barfly in Camden and invited a couple of producers from the radio station to come down.

When they saw more than a thousand teens trying to get into the 200-capacity venue – and Ed singing in the car park for those who were locked out – they realised their mistake.

Radio 1's Zane Lowe, along with DJs from other stations, gave *The A Team* air play and it went on to become the UK's biggest debut single of the year, peaking at number three in the chart.

Another one of Ed's old EP tracks *You Need Me, I Don't Need You* was put out as his second single in August and it reached number four.

Ed released + in September, promoting it on a tour around the country, and the record sold more than 100,000 copies in its first week which drove it straight to No.1.

To celebrate, Ed treated himself to a Lego Star Wars Millennium Falcon set and got a '+' tattooed on his left wrist.

The music industry began recognising his work as Ed won Breakthrough Artist of the year at the Q Magazine Awards and the Best Breakthrough Act 2011 at the UK Festival Awards.

His show at the Barfly was vindicated when at the Radio 1 Teen Awards, he won Best Single for *The A Team*.

The venues got bigger too, as Ed performed at the likes of the Shepherds Bush Empire, which held special memories for him after often going there as a music fan.

Lego House was the third single, released in November, and it got to No.5 in the UK charts, featuring Harry Potter star Rupert Grint in the video.

By the end of the year, + became certified triple platinum after shifting more than 900,000 copies.

Harry Potter actor Rupert Grint featured in the video for *Lego House*.

Ed arrives for the 2011 Q Magazine Awards at the Grosvenor House Hotel, in London.

THE + SONGS

Much of Ed Sheeran's maiden album consists of love songs written when he was a teenager. Ed goes through each of the LP's tracks.

THE A TEAM

"I have a friend who works at a homeless shelter every Christmas. He asked me to go along and play some songs for the people there. I met a girl called Angel, who was this amazing girl. I learned a lot about Angel, the unfortunate ways she earned her money on the street and the things she did with it when she had it. It was a very bleak story. I spent some time with her, playing her favourite songs, and then wrote *The A Team* for her."

SMALL BUMP

"Pregnancy was quite a difficult subject to tackle. I wrote it from [a friend's] perspective. It was my viewpoint looking on them to begin with. It's quite a touchy subject, so I wrote it from the perspective of actually being the parent."

KISS ME

"Drunkenly, my godfather got down on one knee on the Tube and proposed to my godmother. My godmother said 'yes' which is wicked. They sat me down about a week later and said, 'Ed, can you play at our wedding? Play one of your love songs'. Or they said you could write us a song. I was like 'Oh, OK, challenge accepted'. I went away, wrote this song and then I played it at their wedding."

WAKE ME UP

"I picked out every little thing about my ex-girlfriend that I thought was wicked and put it into a song. There's a lyric about New Year's Day on Southwold Beach when I made her a necklace from two bits of chalk, which I carved into a heart."

DRUNK

"I was on tour with Example and I discovered a drink that's like squash. If you put vodka in it, you don't really taste the vodka. I was drinking quite a bit of it at a Glasgow gig and the night kind of disappeared along with it. I woke up on the right side of the wrong bed and missed the tour bus."

YOU NEED ME, I DON'T NEED YOU

"When I first started seriously doing music, my management wanted to change me. They wanted me to change my hair colour and to stop rapping. So, I didn't stay in that position and I went independent. At the time it didn't seem like the best thing, but looking back it was actually really good. I mean, I got this song out of that experience."

LEGO HOUSE

"I love Lego, I always did when I was a kid and it never wore off on me. I can sit for hours and play with the pieces. It fits into the metaphoric idea too. When you think about it, Lego takes hours to make a complex design. Yet in seconds, all those hours of work can be destroyed. I feel like it is the same thing with a relationship, which was in a way the base for this song."

U.N.I

"It is about the stage in a relationship when it is time to go to university. Usually both people say that everything will be OK, and it'll all work out. In reality, or at least for me, it never does. So the song is basically about a break-up because of university."

Ed released his debut album titled + in 2011.

GIVE ME LOVE

"It's about a relationship that fell apart and you're asking for it to be put back together. Most people get to a point where they drink themselves into a dark corner in that situation. It's that point of view."

THE CITY

"This isn't a love song. It is actually about not being able to get sleep when you are in the city. I wrote it while living in [London]. It's a pretty basic concept, but I really like the song so it made it to the album."

A BRIT OF ALRIGHT

By now Ed was making a name for himself in British music and was getting recognition from the industry. The singer also sought out new collaborators to write and record alongside.

The year 2012 could not have got off to a better start for Ed Sheeran.

Just days into January, he was nominated for four BRIT Awards: best male, best breakthrough act, best album for + and best single for *The A Team*.

Ed would be sharing the same arena as Coldplay, Bruno Mars and Adele on the biggest night in the British music industry.

But for a man used to wearing colourful t-shirts with baggy jeans and a hoodie, his biggest worry was how he was going to pull off a suit at the big showbiz bash.

You could almost feel his pain as he sang: "Cause I know that suits don't suit me or help me get around" in the song *Suits,* with grime artist Kasha Rae, that was released after his nomination.

But any fears would soon turn into jubilation as Ed saw off Noel Gallagher, James Blake, Professor Green and James Morrison to win the British Male Solo Artist award.

There was even more to celebrate when he beat the likes of Jessie J, The Vaccines and Emeli Sande to win best British Breakthrough Act.

To top it off, Ed took to the stage with his trusty guitar to perform an emotional live performance of *Lego House* at the glittering awards do, held at London's O2 Arena.

Seeing it as a potential route into the US market, Ed reached out to Alabama rapper Yelawolf of Shady Records and they recorded a four-track EP called *The Slumdon Bridge* in Los Angeles.

The collaborative work for the year was only beginning, as Ed appeared as a featured artist on tracks with UK rappers Wretch 32, Devlin and Rizzle Kicks.

Drunk became the fourth single lifted from his album, with Ed featuring fully in his own video for the first time. We see a cat take Ed out for a night of drinking to help him recover from breaking up with a girl, played by Scottish singer Nina Nesbitt who had supported Ed on tour.

The One Direction boys had been friends for a while, and when Harry Styles asked Ed if he had any

Nina Nesbitt (above) supported Ed on his tour and featured in his video for *Drunk*. Yelawolf (below) recorded an EP titled *Slumdon Bridge* with Ed.

songs to contribute for their debut studio album *Up All Night*, Ed passed on *Moments*.

Although Ed was never going to use the ballad himself, he played most of the instruments and made sure the band performed it exactly how he wanted.

Ed arriving on the red carpet for the BRIT Awards 2012 at the O2 Arena.

PLAYING WITH ICONS

Building a fan base in America was Ed's next goal. And with his reputation growing in the UK, he was invited to perform alongside some real music legends on the world stage.

After travelling to gigs on buses and trains for many years, the aeroplane was now Ed Sheeran's mode of transport and crossing the Atlantic became a regular part of his schedule.

In March 2012, he jetted off to Austin, Texas, for the renowned South By Southwest festival and had the crowd in raptures with a mega set.

While in Europe promoting his fifth single *Small Bump* – a touching song about a friend who lost her child during pregnancy – Ed met Snow Patrol's Gary Lightbody.

The band's singer was a big fan and invited Ed out for drinks with the rest of the lads after they finished a show in Zurich, Switzerland.

They got on so well that they later asked Ed to be the support act on their spring North America tour.

Ed wrote songs for his follow-up album over the next three months with the band's Johnny McDaid and promoted his music on US radio stations in between the shows he played.

Ed picked up another prize with *The A Team* getting recognised by the British songwriting community at the prestigious Ivor Novello Awards in May.

For Ed, it was one of his finest accomplishments, especially as it beat Adele's *Rolling in the Deep* to be named Best Song Musically and Lyrically.

In June, along with legends such as Sir Paul McCartney, Sir Elton John and Stevie Wonder, Ed got a royal call to appear at the star-studded concert to celebrate the Queen's Diamond Jubilee celebrations.

He took to the stage outside Buckingham Palace, where he played *The A Team* with an estimated world-wide audience of a billion people watching on TV and he also met the Queen and Prince Harry backstage.

It was a surreal moment for Ed, as just 10 years earlier, he was inspired to pick up a guitar after watching Eric Clapton's performance on TV at the Queen's Golden Jubilee concert.

Ed had enjoyed staggering success with his debut album + now certified quadruple platinum. But how would it fare when it was released in the US?

To the singer's amazement, the record went in at number five on the Billboard chart – despite not having a single released in the country.

It was the highest album debut for a UK solo artist on the Billboard since Susan Boyle went at No.1 in 2009 with *I Dreamed a Dream*.

Ed also performed at the closing ceremony of the London 2012 Olympics, with a global audience of around 750 million people watching.

He belted out Pink Floyd's 1975 classic *Wish You Were Here* alongside their drummer Nick Mason, Mike Rutherford from Genesis and The Feeling's Richard Jones on bass guitar.

In the autumn, Ed played his first-ever arena in Nottingham in front of 7,000 people and kicked off his first North America headline tour across the States and Canada to promote his album.

As Ed worked hard to gain a foothold in the US market, he was about to meet someone who would give him a helping hand.

Snow Patrol invited Ed to open for the band on their North America tour.

Ed made an appearance at 2012's Festival Internacional de Benicassim, in Spain.

TATTOO ARTIST

There are more than 100 tattoos on Ed Sheeran's body and they all signify moments and achievements in his life. Ed deciphers the meaning behind some of his ink work...

SNOWFLAKE

"That was done when I was on tour with Snow Patrol and *The A Team* came out. I got their snowflake symbol with angel wings."

LION

"The one that means the most to me is the lion. And it's the one I got the most stick for. They go, 'Well what about when you're an old man?' I think I'll look cool when I'm old. I might look wrinkly but have you ever seen your granddad with his top off? Because I haven't. The reason I got the lion was for playing Wembley, it was my biggest achievement."

WORLD

"The world marks the day my album came out in America. It signified that it had been released worldwide and it was available everywhere. I remember that day."

HEINZ TOMATO KETCHUP

"There's a ketchup bottle, I love ketchup. If I get French fries, I won't eat them unless there is ketchup on them."

'RED'

"This was done when Taylor's [Swift] album came out and my song was on it and did a ridiculous number [of sales] in week one. That was a stamp of remembering that."

TEDDY BEAR

"My nickname is Teddy. I was called that by my friends. But now I'm Ed."

'PRINCE'

"'Prince' is from *The Fresh Prince of Bel-Air*. I got that in Philly. I played in Philadelphia and I was on tour with my friends, the Rizzle Kicks, who were my opening act. I got 'Prince', Jordan got 'Fresh' on his leg, and Harley got on his arm 'On the playground where I spent most of my days'."

JAPANESE SYMBOL

"This was the first time I played in Japan so I got a Japanese symbol. I think I know what it means but it might mean something like, 'Yo Sushi' or something."

'GALWAY GRILL'

"It's not actually what I said it was at the time. It was planned for the *Galway Girl* video, Saoirse Ronan didn't play the prank on me. Basically, the video is from my point of view. Saoirse takes me into a tattoo parlour and was meant to write down 'Galway Girl' and I thought wouldn't it be funny if she wrote something different. She came up with 'Galway Grill' and we had it done. I think it's funnier to say the story is she f*cked the tattoo up but that isn't actually the story."

PINGU

"I got that with Harry Styles, kinda like a 'bro' tat. I mentioned it and he was like, 'Go on then'. *Pingu* is a child's TV programme."

BOXING GLOVES

"I sold out Madison Square Garden three times so I got three boxing gloves. My granddad was a boxer and my dad always said when you make it in America, you play Madison Square Garden."

MOTHER AND CHILD

"This one is by [my mum's favourite] artist Henri Matisse and it's of a mother and child. It was the first thing I bought with a pay cheque for my mum – his drawing of a mother and child – and I got this to symbolise her."

'MEOW'

"I tattooed a paw on the arm of a TV host [Phoebe Dyksta] in Canada while we were on screen. Afterwards I felt bad that I had obviously inked her skin and she wrote this out on mine. I said she could write anything."

IT'S TAYLOR MADE

Breaking into the US market would always be a challenge for Ed. But his prospects were boosted when he was invited to support Taylor Swift on tour and they ended up becoming best friends.

Ed Sheeran did his chances of cracking the US no harm after forming an unlikely friendship with singing sensation Taylor Swift.

Her manager had watched Ed at a show in Nashville and Taylor was so intrigued by *Lego House* that she got in touch with him to write on her forthcoming *Red* album.

They spent time hanging out and wrote songs, including the duet *Everything Has Changed*, which was included on her record.

When *Red* was released in October 2012, it went straight to No.1, selling more than a million copies in the US in its first week alone.

The pair had built up such a rapport that Taylor invited Ed to open for her on the pop-country singer's 2013 North America tour.

Ed had planned to take six months off to write his new album – but he knew this stadium tour in front of new audiences would increase his profile and help him break the US market.

To mark the occasion, Ed got 'Red' tattooed on his arm to add to the ever-increasing body art that celebrates major landmarks in his life.

The pair's friendship blossomed due to a mutual respect of each other's music, a love of Lego and cats, plus they enjoyed going to parties or eating home-baked apple pie.

Taylor even made Ed a needlepoint with mini versions of each other embroidered on it and a Drake song quote: "Started from the bottom, now we're here". Despite newspaper speculation they were dating, Ed made it clear they were just good friends.

Back from his own album tour of North America, Ed released the sixth and final single *Give Me Love* from + in November.

With One Direction working on their next album *Take Me Home*, Ed gave the world's biggest boy band his songs *Little Things* and *Over Again* for it.

Written with his friend Fiona Bevan when he was 17, *Little Things* was the band's second single from the record and it became their second UK No.1.

Ed performed *Little Things* live with 1D at the iconic Madison Square Garden, in New York, to thousands of screaming young fans.

And as if 2012 could not get any better, Ed received a Grammy nomination in the Song of the Year category for *The A Team* despite still being relatively unknown in the States.

One Direction took a couple of Ed's songs for their new album.

Taylor Swift became collaborator and good friends with Ed after they went on her tour together.

THE FUTURE'S RED

On stage with Elton John at the Grammy Awards and opening for Taylor Swift's Red tour were big moments for Ed. Then playing sold-out nights at Madison Square Garden was extra special.

When Ed Sheeran got a phone call from his mentor Elton John, he probably thought it was for another catch-up between friends.

To his surprise, Elton suggested the two perform a duet of *The A Team* live on stage at the 2013 Grammy Awards.

Not only was Ed nominated at the record industry's most prestigious awards ceremony, but he was also going to perform with a music icon.

With a glittery Elton on the piano and Ed with guitar in hand, the pair performed a poignant rendition of the Suffolk singer's first worldwide hit.

Unfortunately for Ed, US band Fun claimed the Song of the Year honour with *We Are Young*.

On music's biggest night of the year, Ed's parents John and Imogen schmoozed with the likes of Katy Perry, John Mayer and Selena Gomez at the after-party.

February's BRIT Awards saw Ed also go home empty handed after he was up for best British male.

However the following month, Ed opened Taylor Swift's highly-anticipated Red tour in Omaha, Nebraska, where he also joined her on stage for their *Everything Has Changed* duet.

The song's video features a red-haired boy and blonde girl taking part in childhood activities with each kid later collected from school by different parents Taylor and Ed.

After six months, 66 shows, and with a combined audience of 1.2 million people, Ed bade farewell to the North America leg of the Red tour.

In between tour dates, he lived in a town just outside of Nashville and built a temporary studio in the house to write music with Snow Patrol's Johnny McDaid.

Ed next headed over to Los Angeles for the 2013 Teen Choice Awards and won Choice Music Breakout Artist of the year.

A sign of how far Ed's legend had grown was that he not only headlined Madison Square Garden in October, but he was able to shift tickets for two further dates in a matter of minutes.

It proved that Ed could sell out the 20,000-capacity

Ed was the opening act for Taylor Swift's North America album tour.

Ed sings at the iconic Madison Square Garden in New York where he played three sold-out nights.

MSG – aka The World's Most Famous Arena – in his own right despite having just one album to his name. Even his own record label was surprised.

In a different kind of collaboration, Ed teamed up with movie director Sir Peter Jackson to write *I See Fire* for *The Hobbit: The Desolation of Smaug* and the track was played over the closing credits.

Released in November, a month before the film came out, the song got to No.1 in New Zealand where much of the movie was shot, and Sir Peter gifted Ed an original sword prop from it.

As yet another sensational year closed out, Ed found himself nominated for another Grammy, this time in the Best New Artist category.

However, up against Kendrick Lamar, Macklemore & Ryan Lewis, James Blake and Kacey Musgraves, Ed missed out on the award.

Ed wrote and sang *I See Fire* for the hit fantasy adventure film *Hobbit: Desolation of Smaug*.

43

ED'S CELEB PALS

As one of the most popular guys in showbiz, Ed Sheeran has a flock of star-studded mates. These are six of the most famous and Ed explains how they became friends...

ED ON... TAYLOR SWIFT

"We got on from the start. We were doing a similar kind of thing on different sides of the pond and we wrote two songs quickly – one of them in a hotel and the other on a trampoline. It was definitely very fun. We recorded them the next day... There's an underdog element to it. Taylor was never the popular kid in school, I was never the popular kid in school. Then you get to the point when you become the most popular kid in school – and we both take it a bit too far."

ED ON... HARRY STYLES

"It's a weird relationship we have because One Direction just came off *The X-Factor* and were living in a hotel in Kensington. I'd been hooked up with Harry through a mutual friend who I was living on the couch of at the time and Harry was staying on his other couch. Then I remember staying with him at the hotel in Kensington. This was before they did *What Makes You Beautiful*. We started doing songs together, he first started writing, and we came in the industry at the same time and have obviously gone off in different directions. But always once or twice a year, we'll sit down and just de-brief. It's nice to have industry friends like that."

ED... ON RUSSELL CROWE

"I started hanging out with Russell Crowe because he loves getting drunk and I love getting drunk. We don't get anything from each other, other than, 'Let's have a night out, let's have it!'. We get an enjoyment of hanging out. Rather than there's a boost in either of our careers for the association – we like partying."

Snow Patrol's Johnny McDaid.

ED ON... JOHNNY MCDAID

"[On Snow Patrol's tour] Johnny and I wrote a lot of songs together in hotel rooms. We went on writing together in 2012 and 2013 and he became one of my best friends. In my opinion, we haven't written a bad song yet. It was great to work with Johnny because in the past, I've been in writing sessions with collaborators who don't collaborate much."

ED ON... PHARRELL WILLIAMS

"Pharrell embodies soul and he's such a groovy person. Not like Austin Powers groovy, but even in the way he speaks and the way he puts songs across to you. Everything has a feel to it that makes you just wanna boogie a little bit. When I was in the studio with him, *Blurred Lines* and *Get Lucky* were the number one and number two songs in the chart worldwide and I was sitting there thinking, 'I'm sure you have better things to do than sit in the studio with me at the moment' so it was really nice to have that time with him. He's been really helpful."

44

ED ON... ELTON JOHN

"Elton was probably the first person to co-sign my album in 2010 and I didn't really break in the US till 2012. He owns the management company I'm signed to. He's really messed up a lot of times and done a lot of bad things, as well as a lot of good things. He's achieved phenomenal things with his music but also in his personal life done the worst things. He's been heavily addicted to drugs, he's broken up relationships and fallen out with people, but then got to a point where he's now out of it and can look back on it as a better person and be able to speak to me and give me advice on that. He's done everything, so when he speaks to you and says maybe don't do that, you take his advice."

GO FORTH AND MULTIPLY

It was time for Ed to release his second album and he had some big-name collaborators for it. The lead track *Sing* was produced with Pharrell Williams and it went on to become his biggest yet.

Ed Sheeran performs karaoke in a bar, then guzzles champagne in a limo with a group of girls on their way to a strip club.

That was a puppet version of Ed in the video for *Sing* with the human form later appearing alongside Pharrell Williams, who co-wrote and produced the song.

The Justin Timberlake-influenced track was the lead single off his sophomore album *x* (pronounced 'multiply') which kept the mathematical theme going.

A slight departure from Ed's typical offering, the track's up-tempo style went down well with the public as it became his first UK number one.

It also became his most successful single in the US, where it reached No.13 in the Billboard chart.

A lot had happened for Ed since the previous LP he wrote when he was just 17 and this new album was a story of the last three years of his life.

With more experience and influences, Ed believed the songs, the production and even his singing and guitar playing was all superior.

Legendary producer Rick Rubin and Benny Blanco also worked on it and Ed remained loyal with Jake Gosling for this album, put out in June 2014.

Ed whittled down 12 songs from a long list of 70, recorded each song three times with different producers, and picked the one he liked best.

In his next Rubin-Blanco produced single *Don't*, Ed ripped into a famous – but unnamed – ex-girlfriend for cheating on him with a mutual pal. Released in August and peaking at No.8 in the UK, the song became Ed's first top-10 hit in the States.

Osaka, in Japan, was where Ed started his second world tour, to promote *x* at a planned 179 shows across four continents over a 16-month period.

Meanwhile, Ed was a winner in the Best Male Video category at the MTV Video Music Awards for *Sing*.

His next single *Thinking Out Loud* was put out in September and it almost never appeared at all as it was written after *x* was finished.

Singer-songwriter friend Amy Wadge had popped round to see Ed on a social visit and played a couple of chords on a guitar Harry Styles had given him.

The riff caught Ed's attention from another room and they ended up writing the song about his then-girlfriend Athina Andrelos to the melody on his couch.

It was released after Ed had just finished the North American leg of his global tour and it became the second No.1 in his homeland. It was also the first single to spend an entire year in the UK top 40.

The video has Ed performing a ballroom dance with professional dancer Brittany Cherry, and at the last count, reached a phenomenal 1.8 billion views on YouTube.

It received four nominations at the upcoming MTV Video Music Awards, including Video of the Year and Best Male Video.

Ed was celebrating after being named Best Solo Artist at the Q Awards, held in London.

He topped the bestselling albums chart for 2014 in the UK with *x* shifting 1.7 million copies and he was also Spotify's most streamed artist of the year.

Super-producer Rick Rubin.

Pharrell Williams co-wrote and produced Ed's smash hit *Sing*.

46

Ed on the red carpet at the 2014 MTV Video Music Awards held at the Forum in Los Angeles.

THE x SONGS

Ed Sheeran says this album was titled 'multiply' because it made everything on 'plus' bigger. He goes through each of the tracks...

ONE
"The whole first record was about one girl and *One* is the only song on this record that's about her. It was a kind of closure to a lot of things and the end of everything for that first record. It was a closure for that relationship and that album – and the start of the new album and the start of moving on."

NINA
"It's about my ex-girlfriend, we dated for a year. When you date someone, they kind of fall in between family, friends and career, and you don't really know whether they're more important than the career or whether they're more important than family. It's a song about that."

PHOTOGRAPH
"Johnny McDaid was on his laptop, and he had a loop of this piano piece going on and on. I started to sing a line and the song kind of unravelled from there. We sat for about four hours, me making Lego, and him on the laptop, just building stuff and I picked up a guitar and we properly structured it."

THINKING OUT LOUD
"My songs have been written [when I'm in] bad places. But I wrote this in a relationship at a really, really happy point. Everyone wants to hear happy songs, but sad songs get written more because more people are sad than happy I think."

THE MAN
"I had a lot on my brain. I just put it all in a song, left it for a long time and then came back to it. It's a bit brutal, so I don't really know what to say, because the whole song was this stream of consciousness…"

I'M A MESS
"This was definitely written at my lowest point. It actually turned out a lot nicer than what was going on at the time, the lyrics aren't too mental. That came at the end of a lot of things meeting. After that I was fine. Writing it sorted everything out."

AFIRE LOVE
"That was written about my grandfather. He was always the hero of the family, such a cool guy. He had Alzheimer's, so he never really knew who I was. I actually started writing it about two weeks before he passed away thinking 'What if?' and then he did. So it was odd how it came about."

SING
"This was about someone the public may know. But no one knows who it was. I kept that really secret. She's aware as well, because I met one of her mates and they were like, 'Oh, *Sing* is about her, right?' There's a couple on the next album."

TENERIFE SEA
"It's called *Tenerife Sea* because [my ex-girlfriend's] eyes are seriously blue, like electric blue. I thought when you see holiday magazines of Tenerife, that's where the sea's really blue. It's a bit cheesy! Maybe it'll become the anthem for ravers going to Tenerife."

TAKE IT BACK
"The NME wasn't a very nice publication to me, and I was just making it clear that I don't have another enemy, I get on with everyone. The NME issued a public apology and I just kept my mouth shut at the time. So this song is me saying something like, 'Hey! I remember. F*ck you'."

Ed released his sophomore album *x* in the summer of 2014.

DON'T

"The song's pretty self-explanatory, story-wise, it was one of those situations where someone comes across as a very, very sweet, innocent person, and you take that for granted. Then stuff unravels and you see a different side to them. It's a frustration song, I'm saying, 'I didn't really know she was like this, f*ck! You b*stard...'"

BLOODSTREAM

"I'm not a massive drug-taker, but that song was written after an experience in Ibiza and it's about all the feelings that I got from that time. It was MDMA and I fell in love with a beanbag. During it all I felt a lot of things: I felt anxiety, I felt love, I felt warm, I felt a bit weird. And afterwards, you spend all day just thinking about what you've been through."

PLAYING THE BIG STAGE

Performing at awards ceremonies was now a regular occurrence for Ed. He also created history by becoming the first solo artist to play at Wembley Stadium with just a guitar and loop pedal.

Ed Sheeran's beautiful stripped-down version of *Thinking Out Loud* at February's 2015 Grammys earned him a standing ovation from the audience of music A-listers.

Unusually for Ed, he had an all-star band of John Mayer on guitar, Questlove from The Roots on drums and jazz legend Herbie Hancock on the keys, and the set rocked LA's Staples Center.

After finishing his performance, he introduced classic pop band Electric Light Orchestra and then joined them as they played *Mr Blue Sky*.

It was a far cry from an emotional gig he performed a couple of weeks earlier at the tiny Whelan's venue, in Dublin.

It was where Damien Rice had inspired Ed to become a singer-songwriter a decade ago.

But at his third Grammy Awards, Ed again went home empty handed despite being nominated for three awards: Album of the Year and Best Pop Vocal Album for *x* and Best Song Written for Visual Media with *I See Fire*.

He could at least console himself with two People's Choice Awards he had won for Favorite Male Artist and Favorite Album at the Nokia Theatre bash in Los Angeles a month earlier.

The winning feeling continued at the BRIT Awards after he was named the Best British Male Solo Artist and he also took home the coveted British Album of the Year honour for *x*.

Ed played *Bloodstream* at May's Billboard Music Awards at the MGM Grand Garden Arena in Las Vegas. Its remix by Rudimental was the next single off the album and it reached number two in the UK.

Despite being nominated in five categories at the Billboard ceremony, including top male artist and top album, Ed wasn't a winner.

However, Ed collected his second Ivor Novello at Grosvenor House in London, by winning the respected Songwriter of the Year award.

Photograph was Ed's fifth and final release from *x* and the accompanying video is a montage of Ed's childhood taken from Sheeran family movies.

It was on Ed's Wembley Stadium set list in July where he performed three consecutive sold-out shows as part of the X tour.

He became the first-ever artist to play the national stadium solo, with just a guitar and loop pedal, to pull off probably the biggest busk of all time.

The pop star was now in a position where he could endorse emerging artists and singer Jamie Lawson was the first acquisition on his new label Gingerbread Man Records.

Ed headed off to Italy, where he co-hosted the 2015 MTV Europe Music Awards. He performed with Rudimental on their hit *Lay it on Me*, before winning honours for Best Live Act and Best World Stage.

He then added another trophy to his burgeoning collection by triumphing in the Favorite Male Artist – Pop/Rock category at the American Music Awards.

The singer's colossal X tour which started in August 2014 came to an end with shows in Australia and a December 2015 finale in New Zealand.

Ed then declared he was going 'incommunicado' and ditching his mobile phone as he was fed up at looking at life through its screen and wanted to see the world first hand by travelling.

Though there would be no social media updates for a while, Ed gave his fans some cheer when he announced a third album was on its way which he claimed would be his best yet.

Another year and another Grammy nomination for Ed, with *Thinking Out Loud* getting nods for Record of the Year, Song of the Year and Best Pop Solo Performance.

Before he took his music sabbatical, Ed and his parents made their way to Los Angeles for a fourth Grammy Awards appearance. Was his luck finally about to change?

Ed takes the stage at Wembley Stadium during one of his three sold-out performances.

THE WINNING FEELING

It was fourth time lucky as Ed finally won a Grammy, which was followed by a second shortly after. Ed didn't have time to party as he set off for his year-long break from music to travel the world.

He finally did it. Ed Sheeran collected his first-ever Grammy at the 2016 awards ceremony.

Ed won Best Pop Solo Performance for his hit track *Thinking Out Loud* at another star-studded bash in Los Angeles.

He saw off competition from Kelly Clarkson, Ellie Goulding, close friend Taylor Swift and The Weeknd to claim the elusive prize.

And it got even better when he picked up a second gong of the night when *Thinking Out Loud* won Song of the Year.

Competition in this category was fierce with Ed up against Taylor, Little Big Town, Wiz Khalifa & Charlie Puth and Kendrick Lamar.

Now a double Grammy winner, Ed was overcome with joy when he accepted the award from his boyhood hero Stevie Wonder.

He had already won the Favorite Male Artist accolade at the People's Choice Awards the month before but this was extra special.

There was barely time to celebrate at the Grammy after-parties because Ed jetted off to Iceland to celebrate his 25th birthday in the first stop of his year-long break with girlfriend Cherry Seaborn.

Ed and Cherry had known each other since school days and had reportedly been dating since the summer of 2015.

He didn't get off to the best of starts in Iceland as while they were touring an active volcano, Ed strayed from the path and badly burned his foot after slipping into a hot spring.

While away, he and Rudimental were nominated for a BRIT Award for Best British Single with *Bloodstream*, while Ed's *Photograph* got a nod for British Video of the Year. However, Ed was not victorious on this occasion.

Ed received an Ivor Novello award nomination for *Bloodstream* in the Best Song Musically and Lyrically category but missed out. Ironically, the prize went to Ed's Gingerbread Man Records protege Jamie Lawson for *Wasn't Expecting That*.

Once Ed's burnt foot had healed, he and Cherry

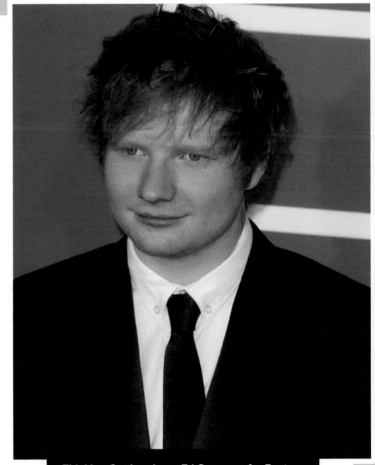

Thinking Out Loud won Ed Grammys for Best Pop Solo Performance and Song of the Year.

made their way around rural Japan for a month where Ed learned to ski for the first time.

Ed was invited to join rock legend and another childhood icon Eric Clapton on stage during his residency at the Nippon Budokan arena in Tokyo.

He released a video – via the Twitter account of *The Late Late Show* producer Ben Winston – promising to eat an assortment of wacky Japanese food if viewers donated to Red Nose Day US.

Ed was true to his word and guzzled the stomach-churning delicacy of sea snails – and while wearing a red tutu for charity.

Ed shared a stage with one of his idols Eric Clapton when the guitar legend was on tour in Japan.

Drum and bass group Rudimental worked with Ed on *Bloodstream* which was nominated for a BRIT Award.

53

WHAT THE STARS SAY

Many of the biggest names in world music love hanging out and working alongside Ed Sheeran. Some of his A-list friends talk about their relationship with the Suffolk pop singer...

One Direction star Harry Styles is one of Ed's best mates in the industry.

ELTON JOHN ON ED

"He reminds me of me when I first started out; his enthusiasm and his love. He's always doing something, whether he's writing his own stuff or he's writing with other people. And that's how I remember myself being in 1970 when I first came to America. It was just all systems go. Nothing was impossible. You're working on adrenaline and the sheer fact that you're a success. I mean, he started out playing people's living rooms, busking, doing all that. So he's paid his dues. And just the fact that he's got the balls to go and do that in front of 90,000 people – that takes a lot of balls. I've been performing for a long time. I've done solo concerts at Madison Square Garden and outside as well, but I haven't played to 90,000 people. That takes a lot of confidence. And he has no shortage of it."

JUSTIN BIEBER ON ED

"It was cool to work with Ed, I think he's one of the most talented writers in the game right now. Just to have his input, have his stories and our stories, being able to match them up together and say, 'What have you been through?' and kind of telling the same story [on *Love Yourself*]. I think it's cool for him as well because it always feels good when you write a song and have someone else sing it. He's cool to hang out with and a really chilled guy."

HARRY STYLES ON ED

"I'm a big fan, he's one of the most talented dudes I have met. Just in terms of his music knowledge, I think you'd struggle to find someone who knows more about music in general. He's definitely a special person, and as you can see from what the album [÷] has done, he's an outrageous musician. It's done so well. And when you're lucky enough to call someone a friend, it's great to be able to see them do something so amazing. I've been a fan of all of his albums so it's really great to see this one do so well too."

PHARRELL WILLIAMS ON ED

"I had a wonderful time with him in the studio and he's really a genius artist, he really is. I think he is the very definition of the singer-songwriter and I think he leads the charge in this day and age as a singer-songwriter. Like it's him, it's Adele. There's a handful of really good singer-songwriters and they're changing music."

TAYLOR SWIFT ON ED

"Ed and I wrote a duet called *Everything Has Changed* while sitting on a trampoline in my back yard. It's a lot easier than you think. We had a guitar, which we passed back and forth, and then ate apple pie afterwards. His performance at the Olympics closing ceremony was incredible – I really think that was his big breakthrough moment. You can't generalise about an entire country, but I like the energy of British men. Ed's such a good friend now – he's just the coolest guy and so much fun. I love that British dry, sarcastic sense of humour. We've got matching Scottish folds, made each other arts and craft Christmas presents, vacationed with our families, and had each other's backs. He is the James Taylor to my Carole King and I can't imagine a time when he wouldn't be."

YEAR-LONG HOLIDAY

Ed saw a number of different countries while travelling the world with his girlfriend. When he wasn't sight-seeing, Ed spent time working on new music for his forthcoming album.

If Ed Sheeran was trying to be inconspicuous during his travels, he wasn't doing a good job as he was spotted by fans hanging out in the bars of New Zealand.

While with his girlfriend Cherry Seaborn in Queenstown – which is regarded as the adventure sport capital of the world – thrill-seeker Ed decided to make the most of it.

He did a bungee jump to get over his fear of heights and even flew standing up, strapped to the front of movie director Sir Peter Jackson's war plane.

The couple then made a visit to Australia where they hired a Mini and drove up the east coast. They were seen in various parts of New South Wales, popping in to Sydney, and checking out the tasty wine of the Hunter Valley region.

Ed also spent three weeks in Ghana where he collaborated with Ghanaian-English singer Fuse ODG on some African-influenced music.

News emerged that Ed was filed with a $20million lawsuit that claimed his ballad *Photograph* copied *The X Factor* winner Matt Cardle's song *Amazing*. The case was later settled.

It didn't stop Ed and Cherry from enjoying their trip to the US where they caught up with Taylor Swift and friends for her 2016 Fourth of July party. Neighbours heard the two singers loudly duet the Britney Spears song *...Baby One More Time*.

The media reported that Ed was hit for a second lawsuit in as many months when he was sued for allegedly copying elements of Marvin Gaye's *Let's Get It On* for his award-winning single *Thinking Out Loud*.

Ed may have been on a music hiatus while travelling the world, but he still had a major impact on the charts. He had given Justin Bieber *Love Yourself* and it became Billboard's number one song of 2016 and was also nominated for a Grammy.

Fully recharged, Ed made a return from his year-long vacation – that also included trips to Fiji and Liberia – and admitted that he missed the buzz of playing live.

Ed took a break from music for a year so he could travel the world with his girlfriend Cherry.

His first gig back was at an East Anglia's Children's Hospices fundraiser in December.

He appeared with an inch-long scar on his right cheek after it was reported that Princess Beatrice accidentally sliced his face with a sword when attempting to 'knight' fellow singer James Blunt at a party. Though Blunt claimed months later that the story was fabricated and Ed did it himself.

Ed again teamed up with Amy Wadge to write *When Christmas Comes Around* and offered it to Simon Cowell for *The X Factor*'s eventual winner Matt Terry.

While Ed was touring the world as part of the 'university gap year' he didn't have, he was busily working on new material for his next album.

And on January 1st, 2017, a year after Ed had quit social media, he tweeted a short video where held up a handwritten piece of paper which read: "New music coming Friday!!"

Justin Bieber's massive worldwide hit *Love Yourself* was written by Ed.

DIVIDE TO CONQUER

Back home from his travels, Ed celebrated by releasing two singles in the same week. They were both a hit in the charts and his new album broke multiple records all over the world.

A rejuvenated Ed Sheeran marked his 2017 return to music by announcing a new album and he took the unusual step of releasing two songs at the same time.

Castle on the Hill is a tribute to his hometown of Framlingham in Suffolk, with the video depicting a teenage Ed and his friends growing up, played by kids from his old school.

Shape of You was initially written for Rihanna but Ed decided to keep it for himself after he felt the Bajan megastar wouldn't want to sing these particular lyrics.

The comeback singles were taken from his forthcoming album titled ÷ (pronounced 'divide') and kept in line with the maths symbol names of his previous offerings.

Ed recorded much of ÷ in a custom-built makeshift recording studio on the transatlantic cruise ship Queen Mary 2 because his US producer Benny Blanco has a fear of flying.

Music history was created when *Castle on the Hill* went in at number two on the UK singles chart and *Shape of You* got the No.1 slot on their double release. It was the first time in UK chart history that an artist had achieved this.

Shape of You became Ed's first No.1 single on the USA's Billboard 100. *With Castle on the Hill* going in at No.6, it was the first time an artist has debuted two singles in the Billboard top 10 simultaneously.

The writers of TLC's song *No Scrubs* were later added to the credits of *Shape of You* after it started to receive comparisons for its similar lyrical rhythm.

To mark his 26th birthday on February 17th, Ed released *How Would You Feel (Paean)* as a promotional track off the album. It got to number two in the charts despite not being an official single.

Ed wasn't nominated at the 2017 BRIT Awards due to his year off, but he performed a brilliant remix of *Shape of You* with grime star Stormzy.

After the release of ÷ in March, Ed was again celebrating as the album went in at No.1 to become the fastest-selling by a male solo artist in British chart history.

It was also third fastest-seller ever with only Adele's *25* and Oasis' *Be Here Now* shifting more copies in their first seven days.

Songs from the LP also dominated the singles chart with nine in the top 10 and it broke another record with all 16 from the album appearing in the top 20 due to the high streaming figures.

All three of his albums appeared in the top five of the chart too.

The record notched the biggest one-week vinyl sales in more than two decades and Ed also scored his first No.1 in the US on the Billboard 200 chart.

US producer Benny Blanco worked on Ed's new album.

Stormzy performed rap verses for *Shape of You* with Ed at the 2017 BRIT Awards.

Ed poses at the 2017 iHeartRadio Music Awards at The Forum, Los Angeles.

THE ÷ SONGS

The idea behind Ed Sheeran's third studio album was to create tracks that were very different or 'divided' and he explains each...

PERFECT

"[In terms of writing] I wanted to beat *Thinking Out Loud* because I know that song was going to define me. With *Perfect*, I needed to write the best love song of my career, and do it 100 per cent me, so everyone will be, 'Oh, he actually can [write]'."

BARCELONA

"It doesn't make a lot of sense. It's just the Spanish words I know put together. There's one line where I say, 'Siempre Vivre La Barcelona', which is actually Latin I think, but it just sounded cool. It means 'long live Barcelona'."

NANCY MULLIGAN

"I actually wrote the song with my cousin. We were in the studio and kinda jamming out this folk song to make into an Irish tune and said, 'Let's just write about grandma and granddad cos they have this amazing story that no one really knows about'."

HAPPIER

"I've definitely got to a point in my life where I'm friends with all my ex-girlfriends now. Like we're all cool and it's very much like, 'I'm really happy that you're happy and with someone that you love'. And they are really happy that I'm happy and with someone and there's a grown-up element to it."

ERASER

"There are temptations out there. A pain eraser is anything from music to food and good company, to the negative stuff like bad women, drugs and booze. A pain eraser is anything that distracts you from pain, so that song was basically, 'I find comfort in my pain eraser' which could literally be anything."

BIBIA BE YE YE

"I wrote a song in Twi, the Ghanaian dialect in Ghana, at Fuse's house with his mates. That was a fun experience because being in the studio with someone like Fuse is just a party the whole time."

WHAT DO I KNOW?

"The song was a reaction to loads of sh*t that was happening last year and I'm not hugely out as a political person and I don't want to be. I'm a singer and I know if I had a political opinion people would be like, 'Shut up mate and sing your song'."

CASTLE ON THE HILL

"It is a love song to my hometown and my friends. Me and my friends have nothing in common other than our love for each other and our hometown, so I just wanted to write a song appreciating that."

SUPERMARKET FLOWERS

"The way that I thought of writing it was from my mum's perspective. If you go to any hospital and visit your grandmother, you will always buy Tesco flowers. It's always right by the hospital."

NEW MAN

"That song is actually not about anyone. I was in the studio with Jessie Ware and I said I wanted to write the 'f*ck boy anthem'. I wanted to pick every single point that you could find about a 'f*ck boy'."

SHAPE OF YOU

"I wanted to write an appreciation song for the female form, like any shape, instead of writing a song saying, 'You're beautiful'. It made sense in my head and people seemed to like it."

A large crowd enjoys watching Ed on an NBC Today show concert in July 2017, in New York.

HOW WOULD YOU FEEL (PAEAN)

"My girlfriend got a cab [to the airport], it was a three-hour drive and I was at home on my own. I was like, 'Oh I'll write a song really quickly and send it to her so she's got something to listen to on the drive'. I forgot about it and when the album was finished, I asked her, 'What's your favourite song?' She said, 'You've forgotten it exists' and sent it to me. I quickly recorded it and put it on [the album]."

GALWAY GIRL

"It was based on the fiddle player in [the band] Beoga, Niamh [Dunne]. She's married to an Irishman, a friend of mine. I had the band in my house for an extra day so I was like, 'What can I write about?' She plays the fiddle in an Irish band... right, cool, let's write a song about that. She inspired the first line but the rest of the song isn't about anyone, I just made up a story."

61

ROCKING THE WORLD

More plaudits came Ed's way as he was awarded an MBE in the Queen's Birthday Honours. As his star continued to rise, Ed headlined Glastonbury and performed a rousing set.

Ed Sheeran went back to his Celtic roots by collaborating with Irish folk band Beoga for *Galway Girl*.

Released on Saint Patrick's Day 2017, the single peaked at No.2 in the UK, with the video shot in Galway and it featured Irish actress Saoirse Ronan.

Ed had to fight his record label to keep the song on the album because they claimed "folk music isn't cool" but its success proved them wrong.

And the awards kept coming, with Ed appointed an MBE for services to music and charity in the Queen's Birthday Honours.

Ed was on the road for his mammoth 17-month world album tour which began in Italy in March.

But he made a special visit to England in June to headline Glastonbury, where he closed out the iconic festival in front of more than 100,000 revellers.

He had come a long way since his first appearance at the festival in 2011 with an audience of around 500 people at the tiny Croissant Neuf stage. With just his loop pedal and tiny acoustic guitar on the Pyramid stage, Ed absolutely rocked his biggest gig yet.

The 26-year-old appeared next on our screens as a Lannister soldier in the *Game of Thrones* season 7 premiere. As an avid fan of the hit show, Ed achieved one of his long-term goals.

In his cameo, Ed strums a campfire song and drinks some blackberry wine as a passing Arya Stark joins his group for dinner.

Ed then announced he is to be transformed into one of the famous yellow characters in a new episode of *The Simpsons* by playing Brendan, who is a love interest of Lisa.

Back to music, his songwriting and impact on the top 40 over the year was rewarded when ÷ was nominated for the Mercury Prize for album of the year.

Win or lose, being included on the shortlist for the prestigious award was yet another one of Ed's childhood ambitions fulfilled.

At the MTV Video Music Awards, in Los Angeles, a shocked Ed was overjoyed at winning the Artist of the Year gong.

The crooner, who was up against Bruno Mars, The Weeknd, Lorde, Kendrick Lamar and Ariana Grande, collected the award shortly after performing his track *Shape of You* on stage.

Perfect was the fourth single released from ÷ and Ed says it is the song that he was most proud of from the album.

He set another milestone by announcing a North America stadium tour for 2018, with tickets going on sale at massive venues such as the Rose Bowl in Pasadena and the Dallas Cowboys' AT&T Stadium.

When Ed first met Damien Rice as a 13-year-old boy, never in his wildest dreams did he think he would become an international stadium act.

The Suffolk singer has already achieved so much in the six years since his debut album + came out.

With so much more to offer, you can be sure that Ed Sheeran will go on to become one of music's greats.

Irish actress Saoirse Ronan featured in the video for *Galway Girl*.

Ed holds his Artist of the Year trophy at the MTV Video Music Awards in Los Angeles.

MAJOR AWARDS

AMERICAN MUSIC AWARDS
2015   Favorite Male Artist – Pop/Rock

BRIT AWARDS
2012   British Breakthrough Act
2012   British Male Solo Artist
2015   British Male Solo Artist
2015   British Album – *x*

GRAMMY AWARDS
2016   Song of the Year – *Thinking Out Loud*
2016   Best Pop Solo Performance – *Thinking Out Loud*

IVOR NOVELLO
2012   Best Song Musically and Lyrically – *The A Team*
2015   Songwriter of the Year

MTV EUROPE MUSIC AWARDS
2015   Best Live Act
2015   Best World Stage – V Festival, Hylands Park

MTV VIDEO MUSIC AWARDS
2014   Best Male Video – *Sing*
2017   Artist of the Year

PEOPLE'S CHOICE AWARDS
2015   Favorite Album – *x*
2015   Favorite Male Artist
2016   Favorite Male Artist

Q AWARDS
2011   Breakthrough Artist
2014   Best Solo Artist
2015   Best Solo Artist

DISCOGRAPHY

STUDIO ALBUMS
Sep, 2011   + (UK 1, US 5)
Jun, 2014   *x* (UK 1, US 1)
Mar, 2017   ÷ (UK 1, US 1)

EXTENDED PLAYS
Jan, 2005   *The Orange Room*
Mar, 2006   *Ed Sheeran*
Jun, 2007   *Want Some?*
Nov, 2009   *You Need Me* (UK 142)
Feb, 2010   *Loose Change* (UK 90)
Jun, 2010   *Songs I Wrote with Amy* (UK 199)
Dec 2010   *Live at the Bedford*
Jan, 2011   *No.5 Collaborations Project* (UK 46)
Apr, 2011   *One Take EP*
Dec, 2011   *Thank You*
Feb, 2012   *The Slumdon Bridge*

SINGLES
Jun, 2011   *The A Team* (UK 3, US 45)
Aug, 2011   *You Need Me, I Don't Need You* (UK 4)
Nov, 2011   *Lego House* (UK 5, US 42)
Feb, 2012   *Drunk* (UK 9)
May, 2012   *Small Bump* (UK 25)
Nov, 2012   *Give Me Love* (UK 18)
Nov, 2013   *I See Fire* (UK 13)
Apr, 2014   *Sing* (UK 1, US 13)
Aug, 2014   *Don't* (UK 8, US 9)
Sep, 2014   *Thinking Out Loud* (UK 1, US 3)
Feb, 2015   *Bloodstream* (UK 2)
May, 2015   *Photograph* (UK 15, US 10)
Jan, 2017   *Castle on the Hill* (UK 2, US 6)
Jan, 2017   *Shape of You* (UK 1, US 1)
Mar, 2017   *Galway Girl* (UK 2, US 53)
Sep, 2017   *Perfect* (UK 4, US 22)

Printed in Great Britain
by Amazon